Perspectives

Stop Wasting Food!

How Can We Do It?

Series Consultant: Linda Hoyt

Flying Start
to Literacy®

Contents

Introduction

Do you waste food?

Most people answer yes to this question. And that means we have a problem. About one-third of the food that's produced worldwide never makes it into the mouth of a human being.

So think about it: What is the best way to stop wasting the massive mountains of food that are thrown away each day?

Does wasting food matter?

One-third of the food produced each year for humans gets thrown away.

Top 5 wasted foods

Which foods are most often thrown away? Here are the top 5 foods that are thrown away, and why.

1

Bread

Over 240 million slices of bread are thrown away each year. People like to eat fresh bread, and this means bread baked on the day they eat it. Supermarkets find it hard to sell "yesterday's" bread because it is a day old.

Milk

About 5.9 million glasses of milk are thrown away each year. This is because there are laws that say most milk products must have a use-by date on them. Many milk products are thrown away if they have not been used by this date.

3

Potatoes

Each year, 5.8 million potatoes are thrown away.

Potatoes are thrown away on farms, in supermarkets and in our homes. Many potatoes grown on farms don't even get to the shops because they are too small or too big, or not quite right in some way. In shops, potatoes are sometimes thrown away when they get a bit old. But these potatoes are perfectly fine to eat.

Cheese

4

Over three million slices of cheese are thrown away each day. Why? Like milk, cheese has a use-by date, and lots of cheese is thrown away if it is left out of the fridge or if it has not been used by the use-by date.

Apples

5

Each year 1.3 million apples are thrown away. Apples bruise easily, and bruised apples don't make it out of the orchard and into the shops. Neither do the "ugly" apples because shop owners think that people won't buy apples that are misshapen.

The good, the bad and the ugly

It is estimated that between 20 and 40 per cent of all fruits and vegetables are rejected before they reach the shops because they don't look good to shop owners and shoppers.

Do they taste different?
Would you eat them?

Speak out!

Read what these students have to say about wasting food.

When people throw away food at home, it might not look like much – but it all adds up to a huge amount of wasted food.

I think that if people have the facts and statistics on food waste, it will influence them to waste less food. Even if it's just a little thing for each family, it will have a huge impact on our world.

Food waste is a big problem. If food is left over in shops and restaurants, it should be donated. Many people around the world are slowly starving. If we donate the food, we can find good uses for it instead of letting it rot away.

Many people think they should have all foods all through the year, which means having foods that are out of season.

Someone might want a mango in winter. When they take the first bite, they will realise it doesn't taste very good – and they will throw it out.

Stop wasting food!

Written by Tess Quinn

You may not do the shopping or the cooking at home, but here are some ways you can help reduce food waste.

Will these ideas work for you?

Don't serve yourself more food than you can eat.

Tell your mum and dad what you like to eat (and not just lollies and fast food!).

Save what you can't eat for later.

If your apple or another type of fruit has a bruise, don't throw it away. Ask someone to cut off the bruised part so that you can eat the rest of it.

How to write about your opinion

State your opinion

Think about the main question in the introduction on page 4 of this book. What is your opinion?

Research

Look for other information that you need to back up your opinion.

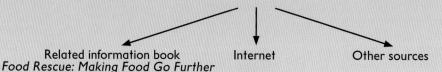

Related information book
Food Rescue: Making Food Go Further

Internet

Other sources

Make a plan

Introduction

How will you "hook" the reader to get them interested?

Write a sentence that makes your opinion clear.

List reasons to support your opinion.

Support your reason
with examples.

Support your reason
with examples.

Support your reason
with examples.

Conclusion

Write a sentence that makes your opinion clear. Leave your reader with a strong message.

Publish

Publish your writing.

Include some graphics or visual images.